Humanity's Reluctant Connoisseur

Becky (Ruff) Reed

ISBN:1479122203
ISBN-13:9781479122202

Third in the Series:
Romance Stew
ISBN – 10: 0978961102
ISBN – 13: 978-0978961107

Life in the Aftermath of a Narcissist
ISBN – 10: 1470106558
ISBN – 13: 978-1470106553

DEDICATION

To all dealing with this entity of a psychopath and the relationship chaos that ensues. This book is the complilation of my blog posts following such an ordeal. We survivors will make it to the other side of this stormy ocean. We are not alone. Although never the same, we are warriors of the spirit.

CONTENTS

Acknowledgment   i

1   Everyone Has A   1
Photographic
Memory...Some
Lack Film

2   The Now...with   7
Gusto

3   Libidinal   10
Investment

4   "If" ~ Rudyard   15
Kippling

5   "At the Touch of   19
Love, Everyone
Becomes a Poet"
~ Plato

6   Possibilities and   22
Accountability

7   Freedom,   25
History, and
Ethics...

8   Letting Go fo the   28
Attachment to the
Outcome

9   Living on   31

Purpose

10   Adventure,   34
      Relationships,
      Ideals, and
      Seeking the Best

11   Somedays the   38
      Bug, Somedays
      the Windshield

12   Every Mind Must   41
      Make It's Choice

      Interview with
13   the Devil   44

14   A Whack on the   48
      Head

      Our Own
15   Ethernet Cloud   51

16   Teachers and   55
      Pupils are We

17   Terminally on the   59
      Upswing

18   Cowboys and   61
      Aliens

ACKNOWLEDGMENTS

With the anguish of the roller coaster ride of existence, I found amazing aid in the form of information from Sandra L. Brown (Women Who Love Psychopaths), Thomas Sheridan (Puzzling People, the Labyrinth of the Psychopath), Dr. Robert Hare (Without Conscience), Sam Vaknin (Malignant Self Love), Lisa E. Scott (It's All About Him), and in the recovery stages, Jon Ronson (The Psychopath Test).Thank you to all of those who rode this extraordinary current of learning.

1

EVERYONE HAS A **PHOTOGRAPHIC MEMORY...SOME LACK FILM**

Life in the Aftermath of a narcissist/psychopath has altered my perception of beliefs, self hood, and my view of humanity and my place. A sense of humor has returned!

Time with a man that I believe to be a psychopath and his extended other-worldly family members, led me from the paralysis of shock in what I had chosen and allowed into my life, through a maze of recovery. But, the word recovery is not altogether accurate. I came out the other side of the surreal nightmare as a different "me." It was as if the naivete of my delicate aspects of compassion and empathy had undergone compression as coal does when forming a diamond.

My entry into this fun-house experience of frightening preternatural behavior began with my marriage; the one I jumped to embrace as I romantically and hopefully expected love in later life with all the trimmings. The relentless surprises from the onset of our marriage, following the whirlwind courtship, proved extremely costly as I worked to bestow balance to the tsunami of needs and never-ending financial crises from my spouse and his family members.

Looking back, I gave as freely as they took; as if there was a replenishing cycle from "on high" that would eternally fill the empty bank coffers. Believing the familial love and basking in my unity with the clan, I jumped as a key player in a trained animal act to supply any missing ingredients to this sad "toxic cocktail" (Sandra L. Brown). The anguish and out-of-place-and-time feel developed from being so quickly used, devalued, and discarded (Lisa E. Scott). I had been no more than a tool of convenience to a traveling troop of grand actors as they paraded across the stage of my life and inner goals.

The goodnesses of decency, love, and sacrifice for the greater picture had been surreally cut from a connection to me, the being, and devoured by the clan as an entree from the menu. There is a skit from the TV sitcom,

"Everybody loves Raymond," where the beleaguered wife describes her dysfunctional in-laws as a "traveling freak show that pitches a tent outside her home." That was my take on the reality into which I had placed my roller coaster car in this carnival.

Two years past the time line mark of being discarded, I have journeyed far within myself as I've sought answers and the ticket office to comprehension. This beast of psychopathy and turn of directions for living left a deeply embedded scar as if I had been unwittingly vaccinated. My immunity from contact with this attenuated organism has produced a state of non responsiveness to this disease of ponerology, the theological doctrine of dark wickedness. But just hopefully I AM still a compassionate, bright, and aware presence.

Checking my email, I found a question from a lovely person from a forum to which I belong. She was puzzled by the "unfriending" of an individual when her response to a post was simply questioning a written thought. Facebook is such a strange land. It reminds me of much of my life and especially that time with a narcissist. Always wary of how I present myself...I find that even two years out, I watch my responses a bit. I like many authors, page and forum creators, and even individual posters very much, however, I think ego for people who have attained an essence of familiarity is highlighted. And the "unfriending" on this social network has struck me many times as traumatic.

Being so "damaged" as I was in the beginning with the psychopath...and truthfully, as Sandra Brown writes because of the attraction for both me with my own baggage mixed with this entity and its need to be appreciated, I have found myself at times feeling adrift. These forums are marvelous, and yet, there comes a moment when we have to be prepared (in my way of thinking) to figure out just who each of us (me, in this case) is on the inside, and how we want to proceed. It sounds so simple when I write it, but it's full of unknowns. I'd like to say I know exactly who I am, and where I am headed, but I'm just beginning...AGAIN.

I finished watching the movie, "Another Woman," with Gena Rowlands, Mia Farrow, Gene Hackman and many other well known actors. It deals with a relatively accomplished woman who finds herself not really happy with the choices she's made in life. That's a bit how I feel. Did I manage to hide it before the psychopath? Was that just the wake-up call? But, somehow in dealing with "putting it out there" for all to see, trying to reasonably assess responses, and continuing on, I think it must really have to do with finding our own strengths and acknowledging that we have every right to be who we are. Unconventional or not.

Sounds simplistic when put down in words. Did we on that "unfriended" list do anything wrong? Perhaps not at all. I do believe that PTSD has affected me...and just maybe all of us. AND if Brown is correct, it's to be a lifelong condition. I used to take negatives from the "ether" so to heart. Now - and I hope I haven't become too much in line with the psychopath's modus operandi - I look at my "intention." I suspect I am now and perhaps forever "screwy." I tread lightly at times with others because I don't always agree - especially as we each are living and picking up the pieces at our own stages and pace. I know I do not look at life as I did in my enthusiastic vivacity before the psychopathic encounter. Maybe that's not a bad thing. BUT, I will say that we must each be as honest with ourselves and our thoughts/responses as possible...for ultimately it isn't even about the acquisition of data to make sense of the ordeal. We are learning to be authentic once more.

There seems right now to be a huge amount of energy spent on dealing with plagiarism. I have written a couple of little books and I make a pittance...but truthfully, they simply allowed me to say what I had and felt I needed to express. I am not those written works. And yet, that is in itself naive because words of valuable impact touch other's souls as the ones writing them reach from their most genuine essences.

Monetary exchange seems always to pack a punch. I not long ago noted a beautiful thought: "the universe doesn't require us to toil."(unknown) We seem to be operating from a place of concepts dealing with exchange. There IS exchange, but it may not appear as strictly equivalent. I am returning more and more to looking at my intent when communicating. AND I find that even with all my faults, absurdities, idiosyncrasies, and oddball beliefs, that I'm not such a bad person. I'm just a plain- Jane human being with no particular credits of fame and right now looking at finding more income within some parameters I have created myself. I have only gingerly toyed with the idea of romantic liaisons.

I am smiling as I remember the movie, "The Mirror Has Two Faces." In it the rather strange male lead wants a relationship of mutual trust, respect, love and he feels it can only be found on the elevated mental and emotional plane of health if sex is not part of the mix. He proposes to his lady-friend, another college professor, and with her prospects for romance with a capital "R" being low to nill - she feels herself to be oh-so less than attractive as a woman - she accepts.

While the hormones remain at bay, she quips to his friend that the relationship is all so " sanitary." As the attraction between the couple grows from genuinely "seeing" the other, the idea of sex becomes less than ethereal and passion begins to develop. He remains afraid to add that ingredient, fearing the amazing zest and friendship will dissipate as in past experiences. She, on the other hand, longs for the unifying adventure where all the walls fall.

Maybe that is what we who find our way to forums and networking sites seek. A freedom of expression and openness. But, the feel of closeness may only be imaginary because we need more than a two-dimensional representation of our humanity. "Faith always contains an element of risk, of venture; and we are impelled to make the venture by the affinity and attraction which we feel in ourselves." ~ Dean Inge

2
THE NOW...WITH GUSTO

My two grandsons, ages 6 and 7, and I beat-feet riding a longer distance than usual on our three bicycles to outrun an incoming thunderstorm. Old Grandma, in my mind's eye, looked a bit like a hippo paddling a storm tossed lake with gale force winds swinging the canoe as I huffed and puffed and pushed to pedal the bike...all the while muttering, Dear Power Above, please don't let me keel over. The little men with determination on their side pedaled with great strides and periodically stopped to give Ol' Grandma a chance to catch up. The dark clouds swept closer and the wind kicked sand and dirt into small swirling dervishes as we strove to keep-on-keeping-on until their apartment was reached. Worn out, but full of the joy of camaraderie, we put the bikes away and waddled inside. They and their mom had been invited to an amazing blue-ribbon resort, The Yellowstone Club, and they were full of eager anticipation for this delightful summer adventure to begin early the next day. With their trip, I would find myself using my free days to handle a few chores I'd put on the back burner.

Following an office cleaning job, my energy levels dipped and I drug myself home to lounge in a hot bath.

Suddenly the pulled thigh and knee muscles roared into raging leg cramps. As I worked with different body positions, I spoke with the Power Above, imagining what the newspaper headline might be the next day. "Elderly women rescued from tub by paramedics responding to the forlorn cries of her two dogs and cat." Not so much over my plight because they have a most well adjusted connection with the All That Is, but lamenting the absence of a thumb to open the pet food cans. Moments later, I was delivered from the agony and climbed tenderly over the edge of the tub. Less than graceful, certainly, but functioning.

The next day I helped pack my daughter and her sons' van and bid them a "high ho, Silver...and glorious adventure." My to-do list of an apartment to clean and two vehicles to detail was successfully completed and I celebrated with six ounces of "hard" lemonade, a gift from my youngest daughter and her fiance. An ace bandage and the alcohol had wonderfully delivered relief to my antiquated body parts. I settled onto my reclining piece of furniture with a small meal. However, the sun, heat and missing a couple of food portions in my enjoyment of accomplishment found me in very intimate coherence with a bathroom lavatory. Once again expressing my plight to the Power Above, I evaluated that I could tidy myself and crawl to the living room couch, but could I re-clothe my bedraggled body in the process with my knickers having been rather unceremoniously discarded. Within a few brief moments, I found enough strength and willpower to dress in a semi-appropriate attire and make my way to the haven of the sofa, promising the Power Above never to become schnockered like that again.

Vernon Howard states that living in the Now is being mindful of actions and thoughts that we so often slot as running on autopilot. He suggests being aware of even the smallest styles of movement and body functionings. "Watch yourself as you turn the door handle, walk, and follow through with tasks." The same is true for conceptions. James Allen wrote an amazing work called <u>As A Man Thinketh</u>. People "themselves are makers of themselves by the thoughts they choose and encourage. The sum of a man's thoughts are his character and character influences the conditions and circumstances of his life."

So this "now" should be experienced as new with each passing segment of time. Awareness of this amazing biological machine and the challenges of this physical domain keep the spirit alert. We really are connected to a grand Universe and there exists a large scale map with an overview. Gabriele in the movie, "The Prophecy," has returned to his path as an angel and says to the hero of the third in the series, "there is a plan...get used to it." I love this set of movies. Enjoy this now...it is a spectacular bestowal of Grace.

"I went to the bookstore and asked the saleswoman,
'Where's the self-help section?'
She said if she told me, it would defeat the
purpose."
~George Carlin

3

LIBIDINAL INVESTMENT

Working on my own path in this old world, I had an experience with a spouse I believe to be a psychopath and his nutter-clan. Why the categorization? The definition and offshoot emotions explain my state of present mind and the ordeal from which I am "recovering." What an odd word, "recovering." Because in reality, it was simply a well placed and powerful wake-up call to reclaim and restate myself.

Scientology in my family and extended family members brought the awareness of this belief system to me. MUCH of the data and processes do work. Having said that, I feel that power and a segregatory element of socialization offers a rather well-tread path of control. We all want to belong, to find that brotherhood of like minds. And we seem to desire a connection with decency, on the whole. I watched a very interesting interview with Jason Beghe on his experiences in Scientology, and he has now departed that organization. He made a rather remarkable observation, one that hit home: many of us get involved to help others. His physical affectations and choice of colorful adjectives in the interview reminded me so of myself when attempting to fathom what happened to me in the aftermath of a narcissist/psychopath in my recent history. He repeated numerous times the statement, "I just don't get it." He was speaking of many levels...most of all, I suspect, of what went wrong. Where did the ideals fall short? How did that drive to be of service to humanity take a surreal fork in the road? Where did loyalty to the organization (or in my case, the clan) override the desire to aid mankind? Why did a choice have to be made and why couldn't the call to help humanity fit with the goals of the organization?

One of Hubbard's famous ideas is that of the "stable datum" - the principle that confusion sits at the base of uncertainty and insecurity of self must be reached. Too much information brings a condition of disordered thoughts and a hodgepodge of reactions because the initial point of questioning the unknown part was not comprehended. I agree with this. In dealing with the aftermath of horrific upset, many of us mortals find ourselves on shaky terrain because our own beliefs and place of being finds us in less than grounded territory. Our visions seemed tilted and the directions we took to engage in actions and group connectivity faltered. We felt that communication had been in play and that our highest interests of kinship with the attraction of community had found agreement with "reality." But, not just any reality, the entity or substance from cumulative choice and like beliefs.

And therein lies the rub. To maintain this "reality-entity" one must offer his own thought processes to the alter of agreement, all for the common good. Doctrines keep that definition of the "common good" in line with group leadership's belief systems. Perspective determines the outcome. This is no doubt the reason for our confusions when we assign ourselves to collectives. Even within the smaller aggregations of families, we find that our feathers are ruffled, on the lower end of the emotional upset scale, and our worlds of personal ethics blasted on the highest levels of anguish in colliding beliefs.

Fear of loss tends to keep us in place; even in the very groups which were joined with the hope that *THAT anxious concern of danger* would be put aside in the camaraderie of togetherness. So what happened? As I muse and assess my own life situation with an evaluation of my place within spirituality, I suspect that emotions overflowed the banks of reason. I will give Hubbard his due in that this life and associations appear formatted as a game. The stakes exist as emotional investment.

Just why is emotional investment such a powerful control mechanism? I have the feeling it centers around idealization and the libidinal investment. Libido is not just about sexual action. The definition includes "instinctual psychic energy that is expressed in conscious activity." As we who seek answers take the bits and pieces of the montage of our lives and sort with information from others, this particular definition makes awareness of Hubbard's friendship with Aleister Crowley all the more fascinating. Thelema, Crowley's created "religion," was one that rivaled Baal with heavy emphasis on sexual interplay. This is the reason Sandra L. Brown, author of <u>Women Who Love Psychopaths</u>, tells all to "stop sleeping with dangerous men." Bonds are cemented and the mind will work feverishly to execute a rationale. So, too, in group liaisons.

How and why is this appropriate in my own path of evolutionary awareness? For me, time with a psychopath set a battle scene that assaulted my core belief systems and spirituality of being. Reason SURELY entails perspective. Cause, intelligible motive, and inference along with exercise of mental capacity, all, lay the foundation for sanity. This is a complex weave of life-threads and the tapestry must include not only our own expressive display, but a reverence for differing designs. Diversity should be encouraged and coupled with cognizance of the effects spreading as ripples in the pond.

I am reminded of Ursula LeGuin's "Turn of the Lathe," where the protagonist awakes every time from sleeping to discover a "new reality of life." The world changes each time the cycle of sleeping and waking occurs. The hero is an ethical presence and as he discovers "the truth" of this "reality," he tries valiantly to save the therapist who has at first attempted to aid him, and then began to use him to alter the world for his own determinations. In the end as the therapist finds himself faced with a landscape of charred and burning earth, he goes mad at learning that he, too, is a creation of the hero's. As George Bernard Shaw said,"I never thought much of the courage of a lion-tamer. Inside the cage, he is at least safe from people."

4

"IF" ~ RUDYARD KIPPLING

What happens when a person recognizes that we in this reality are NOT the same? In my time with a psychopath and his oddball clan, I was hurt, wounded, frightened by my inability to understand the unfolding schematic of living, and shaken to the core of my belief systems. Nothing I "knew" and practiced, worked with the setup.

Everything that I shared as a part of a soul which I felt to be generous and nurturing was tilted on it's side and it was as if I had been living in a bubble of protection until this time frame. Many will find my paths of inquiry now to be unsettling and I may even face some denigration for delving into ideas that others feel fervently oppose the depth of humanity. But, the bits and pieces of evaluation find their way to my doorstep of awareness and I am now ready to take a closer look.

I have never been much of a "joiner" because I found that I simply couldn't accept the totality of data provided by various groups, even religious ones. There are touches of amazing "truth" in so many practices and studies. So, just how does one "find a home"? I suspect there is no such thing EXCEPT within our own beings.

My family, including many on extended levels, was deeply involved with Hubbard's teachings in my youth, but there were also blatant upsets from the experiences of those departing the organization. What happened from the time that information was offered and disseminated to the point-of-no return for many who departed that belief system? I have the gut feeling this precipitate turned on the very point of this study: to teach one NOT to be a blind follower.

Looking back to my romantic zest for finding "Mr. Right," I sought more than just that connection. I hoped to find a special niche and to effectively "belong." I did not succeed. Perhaps THAT is the inscrutable test. If as in the short story, "The Turn of the Lathe," by Ursula LeGuinn, we are our sole creators, then just what is it that we seek? Are these pains to connect part of the memory of what we truly are?

I can comprehend those who suspect "Illuminati" contributions to this realm of life. Whatever avenues of mysterious endeavor may open themselves, ultimately, how are we to live in this here and now...and why would it matter? The cute movie, "Groundhog day," shows one man's choices and effects when "there is no tomorrow" and there appears no consequence for actions taken. But there ARE important intents and repercussions to the use of personal power.

I'd like to have a clear cut pathway and plotted course to offer not only myself, but others. I just don't feel it works that way. There are no simple and clearly excavated passageways. Life for those who are more than flesh and bone requires risk and bringing all the spirituality of beingness to bear. Peril exists and I am reminded of Carl Sagan's thoughts that we might not wish to meet the aliens to whom we send our welcome to Earth messages. Maybe naivety is the necessary ingredient for the explorer in us. In the journeys of discovery we must always be accountable to that unique gift combination of ethics, integrity, and honor.

My search from my present platform will be different than the one I find farther down the road. Who will I be? Something inside me underscores that the pathway is essential. I think Rudyard Kipling says it well: "IF"...

"If you can keep your head when all about you
Are losing theirs and blaming it on you,
If you can trust yourself when all men doubt you,
But make allowance for their doubting too;
If you can wait and not be tired by waiting,
Or being lied about, don't deal in lies,
Or being hated, don't give way to hating,
And yet don't look too good, nor talk too wise:
If you can dream - and not make dreams your
master;
If you can think - and not make thoughts your
aim;
If you can meet with Triumph and Disaster
And treat those two impostors just the same;
If you can bear to hear the truth you've spoken
Twisted by knaves to make a trap for fools,
Or watch the things you gave your life to
broken,
And stoop and build 'em up with wornout tools:
If you can make one heap of all your winnings
And risk it on one turn of pitch-and-toss,

And lose, and start again at your beginnings
And never breathe a word about your loss;
If you can force your heart and nerve and sinew
To serve your turn long after they are gone,
And so hold on when there is nothing in you
Except the Will which says to them: 'Hold on!'
If you can talk with crowds and keep your
virtue,
Or walk with kings - nor lose the common
touch,
If neither foes nor loving friends can hurt you,
If all men count with you, but none too much;
If you can fill the unforgiving minute
With sixty seconds' worth of distance run -
Yours is the Earth and everything that's in it,
And - which is more - you'll be a Man my son!"

5

"AT THE TOUCH OF LOVE, EVERYONE BECOMES A POET" ~ PLATO

My cousin writes and is part of a blog, http://fourfoxesonehound.wordpress.com/. We have shared thoughts, our treks with self-education and choice, and we have remained friends with our differing styles and perspectives. As I look back over the last two years, being "set free" by the psychopathic ex-spouse and his clan with their never ending black hole of needs and financial crises when my usefulness ended, I see that I really "have come a long way, Baby."

Just why DO I write? Part of the reason is to share my journey - a bit of altruism? yes, but also to "air my side" of the recovery process. And then, there exists that marvelous gift of journaling: to become clearer on beliefs, experiences, and who I have become over time. A touch of awareness gently breezed past me when my youngest grandson of six told me of a dilemma he found in his life. His single mom's boyfriend had given him a bike that the boyfriend's son had outgrown and it is a HONEY - camouflage green with "cool handlebars" and

I can see his mind of imagination churning as he rides it, meshing his present moment with the colors and grand adventures of the resourceful mental images which he blends with his feelings of daring-do.

The difficult decision? I had also given him a racer's bike with blazing orange wheel rims and refitted to update with safety items such as new handle grips, petal pads, and tires. He thought that the gentleman told him he needed to have only one bicycle at his apartment and that the fellow would take the camouflage bike back to his place. My remarkably wonderful grandson looked at me with big brown eyes as I imagine King Solomon must have faced in the past. The first emotion that bubbled up was one of a territorial sense of indignation. The next was anger that a "gift" had strings attached. My hackles shot into high gear and the battle gear automatically unfolded, as if I were some amazing super-heroine   of   film   fame.

And, finally, I looked at that magnificent presence who felt comfortable enough to share his concerns with Grandma.

Whatever the gentleman had actually told my grandson and his thoughts and intentions, I cared about my young person's development, his heart and soul, and his integrity in dealing with this old world. Of course I assured him he could keep the "orange avenger" at my house. And then ushered him along with his older brother to the glorious speeds and worlds of enchantment as they rode down the way, smiling with eyes shining and seeking the newest childhood exploits.

It occurred to me as I thought about this later that there exists a difference between "being OK with a situation" and "allowing the situation to be as it is", whatever that might be. What in the world does that mean? If one can accept that something is "as it is," choice remains viable. You don't have to like or agree with it and that problematic picture may just not suit or sit well. But, if one can let go of the burning desire to "make it better or correct" by some method, then, you really do have a direction for reason. The situation loses its power to affect your emotional state and whatever decisions evolve from the encounter, the status of that prick to personal ego was but a moment in time. Ah, wisdom...where were you when I was in the depths of self-doubt and heartache? I agree with Robert Frost's quote," I'm against a homogenized society, because I want the cream to rise."

6

POSSIBILITIES AND ACCOUNTABILITY

I have been fascinated by the Katie Holmes/Tom Cruse divorce developments and the connection to Scientology. My close family members were once keenly involved in the technology and rising on "the bridge" of this looking glass thread of reality creation. Although some became power mongers and slid past the idea of the dynamics of connectivity and responsibility, believing that their superiority altered personal ethics and permitted them to abuse relationships, others remained faithful - quietly so - to the tech, itself.

 I remember the definitive lines of ostracization with the "wog" world because those of us "lesser beings" were not of the same caliber. Nonetheless, I found and still find amazing cognizance, skill, and power within the teachings of dealing with this world and its many presences. The communication techniques alone stood me in terrific stead UNTIL I ran into a psychopath and his oddball clan. In truth, even during this period, the methods were valid - especially the "choice to communicate or not." Unfortunately, I became stuck in the need to "right the scenario" and have a "happily ever after" ending.

The great gurus of "what if" in the 40' to 50's - Napoleon

Hill, Emmet Fox, Norman Vincent Peale, Ernest Holmes, Claude Bristol, and numerous sci-fi authors - have touched my being and offered doorways for comprehension of others, but most auspiciously, of myself. Jim Channon of the First Earth Battalion was the core of the movie, "Men Who Stare at Goats." There are so many portals of "just maybe" that we fail to understand. Somehow much revolves around a huge overview and self-introspection of the rightness of actions and the ripples of those choices.

My daughter posted photos of my family on an adventure to a ghost town yesterday. I looked at my pictures showing wrinkles, lumps, bumps, sags, and antiquity and was at first surprised. Just as in the movie, "The Mirror Has Two Faces," Lauren Bacall's character says, " I look in the mirror and I'm old...but I feel young...like a kid," I can say that I share that sentiment. One of the techniques from Scientology is to peer into a mirror, blinking as infrequently as possible, and watch the changing faces of oneself. Could it be one's familial lineage? Maybe. Could it be oneself through the dimensions of time? Perhaps. But I am always astutely aware of the eyes. And this is now, more than ever, the way I see myself in "life in the aftermath of a narcissist." I am changed. I have reclaimed many of my old - no matter how oddball others may declare these – ideas.

MOST importantly, the fear of separation and not being understood or found within company of agreement has dissipated. My beliefs hold validity for me. And along with this freedom has arrived a kindness in allowing others their choice of beliefs. I still have no blanket answers for this world of reality, but my appreciation for the splendor has sky rocketed.

Many share terrible tales of abusive situations for the soul in their dealings with Scientology, some within my own family. Others remain faithful to the technologies. Some, of course, have joined the ranks of the "privileged" and find that we who struggle and work on our place in the scheme of things may not be deemed worthy. I find myself kinder, less afraid, and more strongly steadfast in my belief systems. I have a feeling that ultimately, this may be the entire purpose of lifetime or times.

Having survived the ordeal of a psychopath, the trek through the bowels of the "Twilight Zone" where nothing fit the parameters of my self hood and ideals, and a coming to be OK with me even if I discover myself island-locked, I am reminded of Ursula Le Guin's "Turn of the Lathe." (The Lathe of Heaven) No matter where we locate ourselves on the growth spectrum, we have the option of evaluation, cognition, emotion, decisions, and awareness that our control is of ourselves. The slippery slope involves others, but the best of us in humanity can be accountable while allowing others their creativity. "It is good to have an end to journey toward, but it is the journey that matters in the end" (Ursula Le Guin).

7

FREEDOM, HISTORY, AND ETHICS...

Coming through this period of life where I found myself immersed in my trials and tribulations within the experience with a psychopath and his oddball clan, I forgot to recognize this as a step in growth. I just read Bill Harris' <u>Thresholds of the Mind.</u> I am 59 and have some awareness of Scientology and the thought-gurus of the '50's. I found the book most interesting and written in a down-to-earth style. It struck me as very similar to much of Hubbard's works.

I find myself in a new stage of awareness of myself as I continue my journey into tomorrow. Meditation has long been practiced and urged by spiritual teachers, writers, and those seeking inner peace. I can't help but wonder, being a science fiction appreciator, if *that* is not our path in this evolutionary platform. In the end of the original "Matrix" film, the protagonist Nero knows he can control much of his living experience, and yet, there comes a sequel. Harris and other authors believe that upheaval is the signal for a readiness for growth, expansion of awareness, and new evaluations. Although even Hubbard's techniques lend themselves to a connectivity to an energy band of more than this plane of experimentation, what if this "mystery" of attempting to master Fate by controlling emotions has us forever trying to "avoid" anguish. And this very angst is the driving force for our undertaking of the set of unfolding circumstances leading to modifications and distinguishable differences in our development.

With all the writers of this period in our history, there appears a strong undercurrent of the cognizance of social dynamics, personal responsibility, and an ethical framework that signals a direction away from the lower divisions of taxonomic kingdoms. Howard Bloom speculates in his book, Global Brain, that man and the bacterial kingdom vie for dominance on planet Earth. If mass-mind and cohesion in the form of love bring the sensation of jurisdiction, just what are we as *individuals*?

It falls within my belief system that we - individuals - forge pathways for acknowledgment of achievement in the same vein as time is compartmentalized by us on this physical plane. We need to mark the flow of our coming-to-know. And just perhaps *THIS* **IS** the point of it all. Bloom in his work, The Lucifer Principle suggests a new way to look at sociology.

In my contact with psychopathy, I have, also - like Bloom, felt that evil may be intrinsically set within the formative structures of humanity. The essential character of an indivisible entity may mirror a god-like presence of compassion and desire for expanding expression of creativity or it may pull inward the boundaries of the significance of symbols of communication. The lovely children's movie, "The Never Ending Story" explores the idea of evil being the cessation of imagination and halting the supplement of a forever moving "more."

As I work my way into deciphering my personal path, I discover that this life must be more than simple attainment of food, clothing, and shelter. But, it must also be more than settling into a comfortable cushion of philosophy. The cutting edge of LIFE, in capital letters, is boldness of conception AND execution. Still, the magnanimity must include personal ethics. I believe we strive for a distinction of excellence. History must be taken into account as one charts a forward path. Perhaps that's why journaling serves such a wonderful purpose: it's history's first draft. Winston Churchill may have touched a chord of truth: "For my part, I consider that it will be found much better by all parties to leave the past to history, as I propose to write that history myself."

8
LETTING GO OF THE ATTACHMENT TO THE OUTCOME

Revolutioniz.com likes to say that shaking life up a bit with new paradigms of thought tends to open doorways to a touch of chaos as one begins the trek. I'd have to add an "amen" to this one. I suddenly and quietly came to an awareness - or rather, had one gently wash over me: Letting go of the "attachment to the outcome" brings amazing freedom and allows one (me!) to stretch my boundaries of "what if's." The insane asylum of my past marriage with a narcissist/psychopath and his oddly highlighting clan, will be a part of my life and thinking patterns - and this is actually a good point of reality. It mandates a little clarity be undertaken regarding belief in choice, responsibility, accountability, and the freedom to start, stop, and change (Hubbard).

Time is such a fascinating tool. However we accept the premise of this compartmentalized aspect of creativity, whether "it" exists or serves only to illustrate and measure change, some formatting of this concept is required to witness the expression of altered living energy from the idea state to the physical playing field. As I am becoming clearer on my own deliberations about belief and power in the process of innovative imagination that we call "life," I recognize amazing energy. I'd like to smile boldly and state that I "get it." Unfortunately, I don't grasp the formula and schematics totally; however, I do feel the power and sense the accumulated possibilities that are so close and yet, remain just beyond reach .

In my own experiences, Time appears to need mindful lucency and almost two-weeks to bring a wish to fruition on this plane of reality. Maybe this is a type of sieve and filtering system to allow each of us to evaluate our choices before they manifest. As my personal development continues in the aftermath of the upsetting awakening to the portrait of my life journey with many a bump along the way, I recently had my laptop fail to return from the land of black screen death, my antiquated PC tower valiantly attempt to reboot all to naught, and my ancient automobile simply stopped, as if to say, that's all there is. I might have collapsed into a puddle of angst, fear, and utter frustration, but I didn't - there was a momentary flash of fear...but then there was "thought."

The help of my daughters, son-in-law, and tremendous generosity of my brother and his wife flew in as some invisible super heroes to offer aid. These people opened their hearts, wallets, use of vehicles, and compassion - without maudlin sympathy. Suddenly I experienced a wave of the sense that I was not only "worthy" and valuable in my meager way, but that I had touched the template of something grand and astonishing. Emotions - so many in the lower ranges of my experience within the Stockholm syndrome of my marriage and feelings of utter loss, apprehension, and alarm that my beliefs may not have been valid - seem to serve as a tether to particular states of being and the stronger the band of feeling, the tighter the chord binds one to that place and state.

In an episode of an old "Star Trek," Spock, Capt. Kirk, and some other comrades were trapped in an energy field. Spock who could dampen the projected expanse of his energies (especially fear in the fight-or-flight mode), was the one to decrease the intensity of the prison's dynamic power fluctuations and pass through the barrier to freedom. Looking at Vedic philosophy, there always exists choice of pathway. If I understand the knowledge of this terrain, repercussions don't really exist when one is "on the path of enlightenment." The struggles and points of "re-do" occur only when ego and emotional attachment take place.

Oddly, the wisdom remains freely available, but the student grasps it only when he is ready to release old ideas of self and "shoulds." Gratitude accompanies me along my own walk today. Melodie Beattie states it so well: "Gratitude unlocks the fullness of life. It turns what we have into enough, and more. It turns denial into acceptance, chaos to order, confusion to clarity. it can turn a meal into a feast, a house into a home, a stranger into a friend. Gratitude makes sense of our past, brings peace for today, and creates a vision for tomorrow."

9
LIVING ON PURPOSE

A relatively lazy day and Father's Day found me with free time - after household chores, thoughts on expanding my business, application for a car loan, and a short drive through my picturesque town with my youngest daughter. I decided to watch a DVD I stumbled across at the library a couple of days ago, "The Diving Bell and the Butterfly."

This is an autobiographical account of how utterly dramatically, drastically, and with lightning-quick speed life can change within the parameters of moments. Jean-Dominique Bauby pushed that velocity envelope at the age of 44 when, as a well liked and valued editor of the high profile "Elle" magazine, he succumbed in life's mid-stride to a rare stroke attacking his brain stem. Awakening from the 20-day coma to a body completely paralyzed except for his mind and the ocular movement of his left eye, he strained with undaunted effort and spirit to keep alive his wit, style, and impassioned approach to the distinctive quality of his soul. He continued his grand adventures of this lifetime through his kaleidoscope spectrum of personal imagination and produced the manuscript by using a system of blinking to each letter of the alphabet read to him.

By connecting exquisitely with the vast array of sensations within his memory, he linked not only to himself but to the world around him. He thrilled to life fully expressed, his children, love, and the passionate embracing of choice and opportunity. The tale is poignant, bitter sweet, and ineffably overpowering as a testament of conviction for living-on-purpose.

My own minor - by comparison - turmoil in the aftermath of time with a narcissist/psychopath and his dysfunctional clan left me metaphorically comatose and stuck in a murky purgatory of static existence. Dragging my battered heart, beliefs, and antiquated carcass into a wake-up mode has been an excruciating process of reconnecting to this life. Where once I held impassioned views on interactions, my self-protected cessation of hope and expectation crippled my grip on forging my own role in this experience of metabolic vitality.

Tony Robbins likes to say that man will act more diligently and exert more effort to avoid pain than he will to consciously magnetize pleasure. I find that I personally can agree with this, especially when the anguish comes expressly through the torment of the soul. When beliefs and one's stability of data on individual purpose are shaken to the core, life takes on a mechanical rhythm - much like the life-support for Bauby. The continuum of subsistence shrinks to a very narrow band width and with it, the capabilities of a blossoming presence falter and lay stunned.

After the trigger of a cascade of ideas found in the movie, I wondered "what kept me moving, always with optimism in my past" - before the violation of my spirit? What had left me as a lump of clay? Was it because I accepted the thought that it was "my choice"? I believe I chose to see goodness...I chose to be upbeat in expectation. Now I choose to limit my exposure to self-doubt and anger. Unpleasant, detrimental, and even life-altering deviations from one's path do occur. BUT...

At some point, we can see and feel that each of us are "worthy" of other adventures...higher tone journeys. Those which produce expanded and uplifting proficiency. I also watched "Alien Hunter" this weekend and was moved by the characters portraying wounded people who, for the most part, rose to the occasion of greatness in decency. There, of course, was a renegade being who catapulted wildly in fear and the attempt to escape a doomsday scenario. But on the whole, the staff of the locked-down research facility, who had unwittingly opened a plague that could wipe humanity from the Earth, were honorable and aware of a mandatory sacrifice. In the final scenes, the remaining few were "rescued" by other-worldly presences and we are left hoping that their new trek will be exciting, challenging, and filled with the joy of their uncharted next adventure.

In both of these movies a fear of the unknown reigns. However, overcoming that emotion, valiantly rides honor and the choice to make a positive difference. This may well be our purpose. It isn't what we do so much as the spirit of integrity that accompanies our actions. Claude Bristol's The Magic of Believing is true. So, for me, I will pretend that I am following my purpose of being until I recognize that this is, indeed, the case. As Bristol states, "to win, you've got to stay in the game."

10

ADVENTURE, RELATIONSHIPS,
IDEALS, AND SEEKING THE BEST

This life is amazingly complicated and quite unabashedly grand in it's multi-faceted terrains of experience. Just as I was beginning to see some light at the end of the tunnel I had forged for myself - letting the ex-spouse narcissist/psychopath and his clan forever exhibiting their black hole of never-ending needs sap my entire portfolio of financial assets - my old car died. My niche of office cleaning with a leaning toward special attention to equipment in a variety of office fields, is just beginning to offer a glimmer of growth.

Looking at life in my "later chapters," I felt weary. The trek through the bowels of the Twilight Zone in my last marriage in which I was used, devalued, and so easily discarded once my funds and usefulness as a hired hand and care provider had evaporated, had deposited me within the grasp of a crisis of faith. I have been groping my way forward and this deletion of a vehicle from my present-day grab bag of dealings rumbled the reminder of those devastatingly fearful feelings of violation of trust. Now, I faced my own thoughts of being alone in this predicament. My youngest daughter and her fiance loaned me their truck, having the fiance use his motorcycle to generously share their second automobile with me. And my oldest daughter compiled her Christmas money to be on-the-ready to aid me. I still have the legwork to perform, but there is an air of generosity and warmth. God and the Universe still know I'm here.

The calendar has marked two years away from the constantly overwhelming chaos of changing persona of the psychopath, the tag-team neediness of the invalid mother, ailing father, always present first wife, alcoholic adult son, first wife's drugged-out and alcoholic sister forever sexually in competition with her sibling, aunts who attempted to push me into becoming a live-in care provider for the mother...and the starkly conflicting upbeat expectations I held when entering the marriage. Forging ahead, I find my courage in strange places, and a collage of ever expansive optimistic expectation of living in the time spent with my delightfully individualistic grandsons.

What does this living in the Now for me look like? My 7 year old grandson wanted to go on the Y's indoor contortionist death slide into the pool while his younger brother (too young to ride the water slide) waited below...but he wanted me to go with him. If anyone else other than grandchildren had asked me to take the trek, I might easily have declined. Once at the top of the stairs, he asked me to go first...so I with my round and aged body grabbed the bar, stepped to the edge of the multiple switch-backed slide and just as I was going to let go gracefully - WHOOOOSH! Slick as greased lightning...I went from a sitting position to a flat on my back luge-run reminiscent of an experience with baby oil in the shower. I think I broke "Mach 1" within two meters of the bottom...and I can only imagine the sheer and stark terror on my face as I slam-dunked into the 4 feet of water at the bottom. I was never so glad to see the splashing water lapping the edge of the bottom area of the slide. I didn't black out from G-force, but neither did I breathe. My grandson went another 16 times with me waiting to catch him in the water...moving farther from the end to let him savor his run each time. Balancing the thrills, my youngest grandson explored the deep end of the poor with his snorkel, jumping to me from the rim to add some zest. At my point in life now, THIS is my "living in the moment" with two amazing grandsons that think ol' grandma is pretty spiffy in her reliability as they taste life.

Renewal of heart and spirit can also be exemplified by the movie, "Galaxy Quest," a favorite of mine. It's a spoof of the terrific series, "Star Trek," and the behind-the-scenes' drama with the personalities of the actors, all seeking to find a specialized arena of success, some acclaim, and personal expression and fulfillment. It's very much a reflection of life and coming to validate the idea that we are not alone and disconnected. We find ourselves in high and lower level drama, emotional turmoils and joyful exuberance, favorable outcomes in specific endeavors, and for me, a coherence of continuity in the flows of energy in this duration of human consciousness.

As the actors playing the crew of the Galaxy Quest bash each other over ego and the praise of fans, they also rally to "fight the good fight" and in doing so become astutely aware of the unique attributes of each of them as valuable individuals. The story is one of marvelous redemption of the egotistical lead actor portraying Captain Jason Nesmith, and the powerful camaraderie that ripples from the causal and dynamic change in awakening to more than self.

So, I find myself here, too. Letting go of old hurts and

fears. Rushing down the water slide with heart racing and partaking of the fabulous successes of my grandsons...now and tomorrow and all the tiers above and below. As Jason Nesmith says, "<with> this fine ship and this fine crew...never give up...and never surrender."

11
SOMEDAYS THE BUG,
SOMEDAYS THE WINDSHIELD

Listening to Anna Quindlen on a TV book review program this morning, I found her candid and openly expressed thoughts on this life, purpose, joy, relationships, and always the love of writing to touch a chord of comfortable camaraderie within me. It drove an awareness home. Style, speech, the written word, and character seem part and parcel of the very aura of personal expression. Quindlen mentioned that writers inevitably want to share something of the life force of experience so that another will not be so alone. What an amazingly appropriate sentiment with such an uplifting air of decency.

Facebook proved a doorway to sharing my upheaval when I found myself deep in the stark abyss of confusion in the aftermath of a narcissist/psychopath and extended family. Much of the hopeful expectation that returned to me came on the heels of voicing descriptions of my encounter with these vapid sycophants - doing so on open forums proved a test of faith in my own strength of determination and served to validate this excursion as mine. Tumultuous difficulties introduced me to myself once again, but it was the acceptance of making these choices on my own that offered a proprietary air to the mix. In using the social medium to frankly expose sectors of my life in an undisguised method without subterfuge, I had the opportunity to face fear on several levels. Beyond what others thought of me, I discovered that I chose the tone of my writings - how to respond to less than supportive rebuttals on my contributed selections and to accept agreement with a humble touch.

In the course of my treks into an individualized choreography of this flowing existence, I have begun to seek my purpose once more. There are those who posture and present personas as they struggle to comprehend the inscrutable fallout from picking a door on this unusual game show of life. The upset may settle in the fastidious hope while turning the knob and then soon recognizing that the entryway held specters and goblins.

I find that I robustly desire to nurture a resonating spirit of being worthy. I choose to be a better becoming self. That doesn't mean that the "keys to the Kingdom" fall gently into my waiting hands. Working in self-employment has brought me onto the shore of those who tend to take advantage. It's not always under the umbrella of conscious knowledge for those who desire to wring that last inch from a generous offer. How much responsibility sits on our shoulders? I am not the same person I once was before time with that clan of ever-draining black hole of needs. Responding with "no" can be processed with a bit of kindness and even class.

And that quality of integrity is my goal for myself. William Foster reflects quite aptly on this, "Quality is never an accident; it is always the result of high intention, sincere effort, intelligent direction and skillful execution; it represents the wise choice of many alternatives." This relationship with self is a remarkable entity in its own right. Although we are each more than the accumulation of our assets, traits of character, and choices, this crucible of living pushes us to desire a sounder mix along with more than a whisper of intuitive link to the ether beyond ourselves.

What I am finding to be true is the incorporation of energies from others in our sphere shades the functionality of the crucible. To be valuable, the vessel must be melt-proof and the high temperature chemical reactions of difficult trials within the container cannot alter the core structure. There is not a point of no-return for the spirit of us. However, choice of direction will occur from a self-determined platform or by default. I choose sovereignty over my own lines in this high adventure dramatic work..

I think we are all children in this quest for expression of beingness. Erma Bombeck sums life so very well: "All of us have moments in our lives that test our courage. Taking children into a house with a white carpet is one of them."

12

"EVERY MIND MUST MAKE IT'S CHOICE BETWEEN TRUTH AND RESPOSE. IT CANNOT HAVE BOTH." ~ RALPH WALDO EMERSON

I've noticed a "growing out of ideas" lately and it indicates, I'm quite sure, a new phase of personal growth and accountability. Sometimes this mandates a "changing of the guard" in dealing with connections to others and situations. With all our teachings regarding kindness and compassion toward others, it feels as if we might be working at cross purposes to let certain folks and choices of circumstances move to a distance.

However, energy of a mental and spiritual level needs to experience an unfettered state. The choices of ideas and emotions are self-fulfilling when talking about manifesting a particular path in this lifetime. With my "life in the aftermath" of a narcissist/psychopath, I've taken stock of myself - my actions, my in-actions, the direction I wish to travel in my life now, and the emotions I wish to experience on a regular basis.

Life has her ups and downs and no one genuinely wishes to spend every moment in serenity, but there is a place within the mind and heart that decides - at some point - that this life means something. Something more than constant melodrama...that it can be remarkable on whatever level of staging that might present. That uncommon production played for no desire of public notice, but a tether to the inner landscape of ethical presence. And, this is choice.

Choice, itself is the selection of the awareness of a path. It may not be the ability to buy the ticket to that departing train at that very instant, and yet, this determination has already shifted viewpoints. With choice we head into the realm of "what if." In this frame of reality, we as people seem to look at "investigative evaluation" as mandating communication with others and cultivated connections from like-minded folks as an affirmation of agreement. We don't really need that agreement.

There are dynamics at play and when we intuitively follow the course which leads to the higher ground of decency, we find that life looks better... it actually IS better for ourselves and those in connection to us...as ripples in a pond moving outward. We touch those in our immediate vicinity...social groups...and humanity....and just maybe we move into an effect on a wholeness of permeating energy.

This letting go is difficult. Growth isn't something one drifts into, it requires courage of spirit. "It's no longer a question of staying healthy. It's a question of finding a sickness you like." (Jackie Mason) - With a grin I say, life's a lot like that! I'm working on my Now.

13

INTERVIEW WITH THE DEVIL

I just read the latest publication of Napoleon Hill that was set aside over 80 years ago, <u>Outwitting the Devil</u>, the Secret to Freedom and Success. In the two years following my trek into the "bowels of the Twilight Zone," I sank into the quicksand of a self-sustaining process with a narcissist/psychopath and his clan. I found myself buoyed in a current of some strange delusion of life and hoping that somehow I could be saved. I had no idea where or how that might arise as an agonizing crisis of faith had thrown a veil of unhappiness over me.

As described in Hill's book, I had "drifted away from self-determinism without purpose or a plan...this was procrastination" as I put reaching definite decisions on a back burner. Fear is an awesome presence. We pretend it has no influence over our thought patterns but we carry the stressful worry of criticism...that we might have failed, that we were not and may not be up to the task of creating a positive and happy life, and that we are somehow less than we hoped.

The book, <u>Outwitting the Devil</u> , states so powerfully
that "drifters of thought and thinking patterns cry that
the world has run dry of opportunities, but non-drifters
do not wait for opportunity - they create these." Within
the pages of the book, an interview between the author
and the Devil is taking place. It's reminiscent of C.S.
Lewis' The Screwtape Letters.   The Devil's great
concern is that real thinkers may appear on earth... and
they would share with others the "greatest of all truths -
that the time spent fearing something would, if reversed,
give mankind all he wants in the material world and
save him after death." The problem exists as more than
choice of thoughts. One must be repetitive to the point
of establishing an ongoing rhythm that flows without
effort. This rhythm is the "last stage of habit." Drifting
and procrastination are the same practical knowledge.
Hypnotic rhythm makes dominating thoughts AND
thinking patterns permanent.

So, during these two years away from the insanity that
had become "home," I have been floundering a bit, but
also climbing forward. To think my own thoughts...to
be a Don Quixote for my own beliefs...to make decisions
and accept the consequences along with awareness of
involved dynamics and effects upon others, to risk
applying different techniques, and to decrease my need
for the approval of others. This isn't to say that I no
longer find camaraderie of like minded souls important,
but I can keep my own counsel and engage in reflective
contemplation with a sense of something greater than the
smaller me.

Each person, to live with purpose, must intend to awaken to his own power of determinism - cause and effect. The goal that guides the action must also be accompanied by a sense of ethical responsibility. Discernment is part of this knowledge with judgment. So, Hill's phrase "how to fail successfully" makes a great deal of sense. We can learn from adversity. There is a difference between temporary defeat and failure. To work the system of creative energy, one needs passion, talent, high level associations, choosing to take right actions, and faith. Described as the "stronger sister of hope," (Emmet Fox) faith is definiteness of deliberate aim backed by the belief in the accomplishment of the objective.

And yet, we humans require a payment to ourselves and that comes in the form of happiness. Because there are exchanges in this energy-web of living, one of the best ways to discover personal joy is to find a service to provide. There is a harmony that evolves from developing a purpose in one's own mental, spiritual, and physical landscape. As you gain a discipline over yourself, thoughts, controlling influences, and awareness of repercussions, one feels a unique power of connectedness. Napoleon Hill used a Mastermind group of admired people throughout history to serve on his "Roundtable" as he imagined their responses, actions, and teaching guidance when mulling ideas and plans. The secret is to grow an understanding heart and rebirth or rebuilding of character as we move into a reality of our choosing. Time is necessary in the sense that habitual connection to life's energies of decency help channel our own growth. Challenges will arise, but if we have become advocates for our own self-hood and establish a set of principles for our ideas of right conduct, we can each feel the exhilaration of choice, knowing there is more than the individual "I." When the student is ready...

14

A WHACK ON THE HEAD...
(YES, LIKE ROGER VON OECH'S
BOOK)

It has been two years since the man I married, now my ex-spouse - quite unceremoniously dumped me. Married for three years plus some time before "the event" of dis-valued discarding, I played a martyr in the hope that I could attain his love and that of his family using that role.

I believe my ex to be a narcissist/psychopath... somewhere on the continuum between the two descriptions. Allowing myself to be used and manipulated and pretty much "left for dead" was a devastating experience with catastrophic financial overtones. BUT I did survive. I have survived...am surviving...AND MORE. I am rejoining the land of living and refocused choice.

This has proven a tough and anguish-filled road to travel with charred and barren landscape of my hopes and dreams as I entered the marriage at the ripe old age of 54. I use the colorful adjectives to let you know the depth of upset into which I catapulted. Life in the clan became a prison of sorts in the fashion of relationship Stockholm Syndrome and although I could not comprehend my part in the grand performance at the time, I did make choices - thinking I'd win "my love" and the appreciation of all.

Smiling kindly as I look at that, I can see that my choices and plans weren't evil, but surely were not beneficial for me and my own needs. I required these two years to replay the sadness and disillusionment and to pull every ounce of emotional angst out of the production within my memory. Time is to me, the GREAT Healer. And now I look at the passage of days, months, and years with energy directed toward a future on this time line.

If Lynne McTaggart is correct with her book, The Field, altering the past exists as a possibility. Perhaps not the events themselves, but the affective viewpoints of consciousness. When the stinging blast of heartache begins to fade and life can once again bring us 360 degrees into our next leg of the journey, how much do we need to "remember" and offer discourse for the "education " of others? I feel that's entirely an individual's call. For me, the past serves as an incorporation of the present me...in a line from the Star Trek movie, "The Final Frontier," Captain Kirk tells Spock's brother not to remove his memories of pain - "they made me who I am today."

Whether people believe that the oddity and alien presence of psychopaths is a psychological disorder or a human evolutionary deviation, we who are of the "believers" in emotional energy and the "light" of awareness will right ourselves. This journey of ours offers the unique characteristic of hopeful expectation and creativity on our own easels of living. We can lend a hand to others along the path and still move forward. Camaraderie offers many new colors for an individual's palette.

I like Nassim Haramein's idea that the blueprint for our reality is written in 2-D format on the exterior of a sphere and our experiences of this plane are the 3-D hologram within the bulb. We have fleshed the map of instructional guide and given it flavor and meaning. So, even if there is nothing beyond this Now, we make a difference - that in itself adds a new spherical dimension as we work on our personal existences, permitting us to create our own spherical realities.

For my present moment, I have found the brain layout viewed in scans of the frontotemporal region to be indicative of "humanity's best" referencing of soul and emotion. I was working on a cabinet and whacked my head in that very area. Life is going better. Is there a connection? For whatever reason along this highway of time in healing, I am once more enjoying the trip. Everyday ups and downs, awareness of the high's as well as tragedies, and a connection to something wondrous makes me feel that "who is doing the viewing" and I are once again riding the current together. It was tough to let go (Jonathan Livingston Seagull)...even of the jarringly desolate landscape...and to flounder down the river of this rushing white-water current. Now that I can breathe again and find ways to keep my head above the energy of this river, I can join the adventure. "Only those who risk going too far can possibly find out how far they can go." (T.S. Eliot) I love Eliot...and I'm home within me.

15
OUR OWN ETHERNET CLOUD

Finally having the gods of the internet smile - or, at least take pity - on me, I have my old 2003 Gateway tower computer up and running quite comfortably. I became painfully aware that I must navigate with an appropriately sized anti-virus program AND that I most assuredly need to increase my computer's memory.

This seemed to equate well and even colorfully to my life experiences over the last few years as I lived with a narcissist/psychopath and his"nutter-clan"...and the years following, dealing with being rather gruffly discarded when my money and service-capabilities had evaporated. Finding myself captivated by my pie-in-the-sky fairy tale - written within my own mind and dreams - of living with a larger family and extended clan, I let down my guard and allowed many a rogue program to enter my sphere of awareness and acceptance, shutting down my natural protective parameters.

Overrun with their black hole of needs, I seemed to believe this sharing of life's yolk was a sign of love and longevity. That came from my floppy disk, "the fairy tale." The anguish over having misjudged the menagerie of characters within the play of my marriage shook me to the foundations of my personal comfort arenas and self-esteem. I "froze" just as my old computer did while downloading and installing incompatible software.

I had been cheerfully oh-so-optimistic before this trek into the ever shifting abyss of gas-lighting and drifting realities. My spiritual side had been tethered to my idea of God and the Universe and I believed in "The Just World Hypothesis." Life over my many decades had thrown a few hurdles and I had survived, returning to my state of being part of a greater whole...and content that life was moving along as it should.

Perhaps my wounds within this eerily odd excursion into the dark side of humanity - or some download of human genetics - arose from my own sense of loss of "the" illusion. To many of us who have high levels of compassion and who partake in that grand Don Quixote quest for finding "true love," we thought this was "the IT" of programs. Our Holy Grail of sorts. When my own world fell apart literally, it was like watching the movie "2012." Of course there was fear, but there was also such an amazing loneliness. Goodness and ideals seemed to have been twisted and turned against me. My finances had been devastated, my emotions battered by an unfathomable storm, and my soul savagely attacked. Melodramatic? Without question, but the emotional landscape with symphonic swells of theme music looked frighteningly bleak.

As the days turned into two years away from the tornado of upheavals and chaos, I found myself seeking that link to God and the Universe. I so understand my computer screen as it states, "check internet connectivity." My faith had been shattered. I was lost. There were moments when I felt deeply and genuinely moved by the tales of Oneness delivered by another, but

my own history of being in tune with this Creator fell
into the background and I couldn't seem to muster those
old feelings of joy and unity.
Aspirations and even gumption that had seen me through
job searches and trials of my past couldn't find a
foothold in the "me" of today. I finally have accepted
that the train wreck of that relationship - so different
from any others - has left me injured, damaged, and
recovering...but, I am recovering.

With all the cloud formats for ethernet use such as
security systems and browsers, I am delighted when the
"history" is renewed and I can find my way once again
in the internet connections. It's a fantastic filing system,
but you just have to know the address for the storage. I
came across two books at the library that unexpectedly
caught my attention, Every Day Deserves a Chance
(Max Lucado) and Where Miracles Happen (Joan
Anderson). The stories within were filled with love and
warmth and stamina. That's what I had lost in my crisis
of faith where I questioned the existence of God. It
suddenly occurred to me that I had "dumped" every time
that kind of "feeling" touched me. I had engaged filters
and a stricter fire wall to keep the associations of sharing
at an arm's length. It seems that I chose to avoid
possible pain rather than risk a grand adventure. These
two books Did reach me...and at that split second, I
began to believe once again in a Universe that has great
bounty.

The gateway of information and emotional connection
changed from a trickle to a rushing stream as if I had
finally decided to turn the faucet on full blast. Well,
maybe I'm not quite to "full blast," but it's a start. And
as with shared data and storage in internet "clouds," I
have once again joined this old world and let much fear

drop away. No longer like Scarlet O'Hara in "Gone with the Wind," with her "I won't think about that today...I'll think about it tomorrow," I can SENSE that it really will be OK. Let's see what's "around the River Bend." (Disney's "Pocahontas")

16
TEACHERS AND PUPILS ARE WE

Yesterday I attended my grandsons' birthday party hosted at a bowling alley by my daughter, their mom. Energy galore could have been the caption for the day.

As in life there may be bumps along the way. Three of us adults - my daughter, her sister, and I - handled the bowling event with the 5 and 6 year-olds, the refreshment and cake with drinks location, and the two girls who really didn't want to be present and kept trekking to the game machines. Activities were moving forward swimmingly when a couple of points to be handled popped into reality. Two youngsters showed who were invited by a well meaning classmate. And the two girls who remained reluctant attendees told me they didn't want to be a part of it, parents having departed the scene.

As my daughter and I greeted the unexpected guests I handled the need for them to bring a parent or a note from the parent telling my daughter they could attend..."and it was so" (grin). Within 15 seconds of lapsed attention on the part of us adults, the two "reluctant cousins" had toppled and gutted a Jerry's Kids candy machine. Two very active little 5 year old boys had exuberantly entered the category for "how much candy from the felled machine can you shove into your pockets?" My daughter, a great single mom, had a split second to make decisions which would involve the evolution of the party and its remaining 15 party-goers. She decided to call the parents of the four "catalysts of anarchy" and have them taken home.

The two young followers were picked up by an embarrassed mom and were sorry...so was my daughter who felt compelled to follow through with the decision. The two recalcitrant 6 year-olds, sitting repentantly at a table for the first time actually within our party group, were met by a barreling bull of a verbal grandmother who staged a fit of outrage that would have easily won an Academy nomination. "My granddaughters would never have done such a thing. No one is ever sent home from a birthday party. It just isn't done! You shouldn't host a party if you can't control the children." Huffing away with the gifts brought, she promised the girls a much better time at a local swimming resort.

My first thoughts were "how can we make this better without playing parent, after all it's only a couple of hours." But as I thought of this scenario, two ideas came to me. I had been such a grandma (hopefully not quite as colorfully aggressive) in my eager battles supporting my grandchildren - a heavy sigh of chagrin here. The other mental process brought a memory of the phrase continually written and uttered by those dealing with the school systems: "where are the parents and training of skills and social acceptability?"

Accountability exists. Yes, so does flexibility. But just how does our culture develop into maturity if no guidelines are set? Well, it doesn't...behaviors must be moderated because we share this social network together. There was no small angst as my daughter made her decision: school connections, seeing the grandmother at her work and at school, how would she be perceived, how would the children departing and those staying respond, what effects would this have on her sons' party and afterward?

The time and ease of passing consideration with 20/20 hindsight would leave her wrestling with the concluding firmness. As for the ongoing party, no one noticed and all had a ball. The owner of the bowling alley helped clean up the mess and right the machine which required no damage payment. The birthday celebration ended with happy faces and goodbyes.

I think about my excursion into the abyss of emotional upheaval with a narcissist/psychopath and his nutter clan and realize that I, too, finally made split-second decisions that would ultimately lead to my reinstatement among the land of the living. Are choices easy just because they fall within parameters of appropriateness? No...there may be fallout. What was the intention of the determination? Was it based on a value of ethical standards?

Finding one's connection to that inner being may take some time and no small effort, but the business of this life seems to revolve around the dynamics of a manner of existence, relationships, and the ripples in the pool that move ever outward. So, this goes out most especially to the teachers - formal and otherwise - within our midst. Thank you. Thank you for attempting to see the big picture while working on life's little obstacles. Thank you for standing fast in accordance with your ethical core. Thank you for changing when necessary to accommodate the inclusion of new information and evaluations. And with deep appreciation, I thank you for caring, feeling, and sharing the intended design of the best of yourselves. "A coward is incapable of exhibiting love; it is the prerogative of the brave." (unknown)

17
TERMINALLY ON THE UPSWING

My charming friend on facebook put a great phrase
together, "terminally on the upswing." Coming from a
Hell in the darkest quivering evolutionary quicksand of a
narcissist/psychopath, many of us as survivors/targets
(Thomas Sheridan) find that apathy tends to rein for
some time after mental salvation. That place on a rock
just at the edge of this other-worldly landscape with
bleak colors and fear tinged outlines, is but the first stage
of ending the repetitive madness of "leaving the known."
It is so difficult to find the delightful push for
enthusiasm. I can understand my traveling journeyers in
this excursion into Hades. This has been a trap for me in
so many ways. I remember a terrific "X-files" where the
two great main characters are overcome by a
neurological chemical while the tree roots and fungi
begin to "digest" them. In their consciousnesses, they
are connected and recognize the peril. So, they free
themselves - or so they believe.

Oddities of "life" continue until one BELIEVES that
they are now living in a self-promulgated fantasy - AND
they are STILL caught and under ground. They actually
must have help from friends on the outside of this nether
reality to make it back to our existence.

Betty LaLuna and her host of camaraderie are "friends."

As from the line in the movie "Random Hearts," (and I
paraphrase here) "Just friends? We are surely friends.
And so much more - because of all we have experienced
separately and together." And finding our way back!

This "return to the living" is a struggle. I find I can rest
in apathy for Long periods...much too long. However,
we reach out to each other...we fill the energy and humor
in this connecting spiderweb of affinity and appreciation
for the beings we are...survivors and however we move
forward, there will ALWAYS be this link of gratitude.

18
COWBOYS AND ALIENS

After caring for my grandsons this afternoon, I came home to watch the DVD, "Cowboys and Aliens." Although not laced with the philosophy and belief systems of my favorite movie, "Star Wars," it did host some heavy-hitter actors.

I was reminded, as I watched the high action adventure tale, that we are the "heavy-hitter actors" in our own lives. The story derived from a comic book deals with gold harvesting aliens who are scouting Earth for her minerals and abducting the citizens to learn of weaknesses within our species. Some gore rises to wring the emotions and the aliens are just plain ugly, non-human, razor-sharp toothed and somewhat faceless gargantuan creatures with no compassion for the life forms on this planet.

Warring parties of the savage West made of renegades, tyrants, the common barkeep, and even representatives of a Native American tribe join forces to battle the alien scouting expedition for if they depart Earth, more will soon arrive. To aid in saving this planet comes a "white hatted" alien who takes human form and eventually makes the ultimate sacrifice of death in performing a demolition "cleansing act."

Spirituality and a connection to our planet serves as a
backdrop for the screenplay and actions of the
characters. Times were harsh, boundaries and behaviors
often crude, but underlying many people existed a
courage and awareness of others, and life in general.
It's an action-packed story and reminded me of my
personal search for meaning, comprehension, and belief
systems after my own excursion through the bowels of
the Twilight Zone with a narcissist/psychopath and his
mirroring clan.

How much a part does spirituality play with us in today's
humanity - if we are as some suggest, at loggerheads
with an evolutionary offshoot within the parameters of
psychopathy? We who are recovering the onslaught to
our senses of the wall of absence of empathy may well
discover that spirituality exists even when religion has
faltered. As with the Native Americans in the movie,
there exists something beyond self in living. There are
rituals and traditions that bind us within the varying
bands of humanity and even when we feel adrift, the
rituals may trigger memories of ages past where real
magic existed (Michael Cremo). This may be enough
for this moment in time where those of us on our
personal quests to right our life paths seek some mooring
point.

ABOUT THE AUTHOR

Looking at my altered perceptions and failing to trust my awareness...in everyday excursions...IN THE BEGINNING OF RECOVERY...

This post deals with my comprehension of my own evaluations and the need for validation as I work with myself on this leg of my journey away from the insane asylum of life with a narcissist/psychopath. In my entrepreneurial work with some elderly clientele, I dealt with a lovely wheelchair bound lady. Just beginning to work with her as a bath aide, I was shocked and a bit shaken by a sudden change in her strength as I transferred her from wheelchair to shower chair. As I was introduced to her, she talked of using the transfer board, however, with my first visit which was to occur weekly, I became aware that she could not use a disabled arm for support or pulling motion. She required being lifted from wheelchair to shower chair.

With the second visit, I became acutely aware of declining strength and even a sense of lack of caring for the process from my client. With no previous time with this special person, I tried to communicate with her long time housekeeper who provided transportation, errands, grocery shopping, and general housekeeping but on a bi-weekly basis. I must have come across as addled and my upset was not understanding the situation for the lady and the physical needs that had changed. The charming housekeeper decided she would take the lady to the doctor, maneuvering her wheelchair to car and into and out of the doctor's office. The lady seemed totally upbeat and made the trek with enthusiasm - indicating that my perceptions had been unfounded.

I was stumped and shaken because I simply didn't "get" what was occurring. I share this because this experience highlights much of my "recuperation" from life in the aftermath of a narcissist/psychopath.

Looking back, I finally see that I'm not insane and that what I felt was occurring now makes imminent sense.

The lovely lady had been with her senior companion of an agency for this purpose for over a decade. As I had just begun my work with her, this kind gentleman fell ill and as he continued to come for visits and to do small household jobs and errands, his health sloped into a downward spiral. The lady began to talk to me about her two now deceased spouses, and how this gentleman and she had become much more than the roles of senior citizen and "senior companion." They had become friends and much more than that. As she expressed to me, in another time and place they might have shared a kiss and even marriage.

When trying to evaluate with the housekeeper because there was no family known to me with whom I could speak, the housekeeper felt I was mistaken. And a subsequent trip to the dentist found the lady more energetic with the chauffeuring housekeeper . So, it appeared my evaluations came from no sound basis.

Learning to look, comprehend, and even communicate differently after the ordeal with my own psychological trek into no-man's land, I see that I turned inward, questioning my own abilities to perceive. I sought agreement in some form. And while on this point of shifting sand, I became more emotional. No wonder I appeared as a "nutter"...I sought an answer and failed to understand that situations are viewed from experiential points of observation.

For a while, I wanted to have the housekeeper understand what I had seen, but that is unnecessary. Now, looking back over these few short months, I DO understand the precipitated changes in the lovely lady and that my own compassion and evaluations were on the mark.

Working with the whims of my antiquated computer – dumping, losing files, beginning again - reminded me of my life in the aftermath of the narcissist/psychopath. Starting over. I am surely not the same. Humorously, and if I understand the mechanics of programs, one never really ERASES anything...it is simply over-written so many times that the program cannot be read. That strikes a chord with me. Re-writing my Present and letting go to the best of my ability the "programs I had tried to upload" in the face of my incredulity...and with all my baggage of "super glue traits" (S. Brown).

There is a line from one of the Star Trek movies where Captain Kirk tells Spock's brother, "Don't erase the pain from my memory - it has gone into making me who I am today." I surely suspect this one is right on the mark!

Sandra L. Brown wrote a marvelous article on the degrees of pathological behavior. I find that I, myself, have changed quite drastically in the way I look at life and communicate. It appears from my perspective that all around me are full of attempts to manipulate....especially in the self-employment realm. But what distresses me is my response...and even after all this, I still automatically try to "make it all OK." Odd, because the slightest attempts at manipulation genuinely "set my anger" on auto-run.

In working with elderly clients, I have found many utterly delightful...many who need so much and simply can't afford it...and many whose family members (if well heeled) demand much...partially it appears that they want to "give freely to help the loved one" and for another reason, to appear beneficent.

I recognize that I am coming from a strange land in this recovery. I need very much to work on "just being me from the gut outward." I find that being in a service industry causes me stress and the levels are amazingly high.

Choosing to work with the elderly - because there was a need for this and money available for developing my little business to put food on the table...and a little extra - was probably not the best plan for me, personally. My personality and perspectives have changed after being so used by my ex-narcissist/psychopath's mother. Demands and a black hole of never ending need. So, I am having to restructure my little enterprise...more toward solitary cleaning perhaps.

I heard a tidbit on a Law and Order, Criminal Intent show talking about Asperger's Syndrome. There was much empathy for the "sufferer" and little was told about what happens to those serving this folks. The lack of empathy of the patient is much like psychopathy... It will be interesting to have more data on the interconnectedness of all these illnesses and "stops along the psychological continuum."

In looking at myself in the midst of these little situations - and they are very small, but to me they FEEL huge - I see that I still have a LONG WAY to go in becoming more like the me I wish to cultivate. I feel quite the misfit in many ways....and suspect this is part of the process.

I reread bits and pieces of Dr. Robert Hare's Without Conscience. Sometimes lacking care looks a bit appealing. This convoluted experience and the relationship with psychopaths takes a toll...and it will inevitably take a toll on our social structure and belief systems.